Garfield tips the scales

BY: JIM DAVIS

BALLANTINE BOOKS · NEW YORK

Library of Congress Catalog Card Number: 83-91152
ISBN 0-345-31271-6

Manufactured in the United States of America

First Edition: March 1984

10 9 8 7

GARFIELD'S ALL-TIME FAVORITE
BAD CAT JOKES

 Q: What do you get when you cross a cat with a fish?
A: A carp that always lands on its feet.

Q: What does a cat take for a bad memory?
A: Milk of Amnesia.

Q: Did you hear about the two cats who were inseparable?
A: They were Siamese twins.

Q: Why did the cat climb the drapes?
A: He had good claws to.

Q: Did you hear about the cat who was an over-achiever?
A: He had 10 lives.

 Q: Why do cats eat fur balls?
A: They love a good gag.

 Q: Did you hear about the cat who made a killing in sports?
A: He was in the tennis racket.

 I knew a cat who was so rich . . . he had his mice monogrammed.

 Q: What do you get when you cross a cat with a dog?
A: A badly injured dog.

 Q: Can cats see in the dark?
A: Yes, but they have trouble holding the flashlight.

CRUNCH
CRUNCH
CRUNCH

© 1982 United Feature Syndicate, Inc.

JIM DAVIS   8-16

I KNOW YOU'RE HUNGRY, GARFIELD

CRUNCH
CRUNCH

BUT WHAT SAY I BOIL THAT SPAGHETTI FIRST?

IT IS A TAD FIRM

I'LL SEE YOU LATER, GARFIELD. I'M GOING TO THE SUPERMARKET

JIM DAVIS   8-17

LET'S SEE... I HAVE MY SHOPPING LIST, MY KEYS...

© 1982 United Feature Syndicate, Inc.

DON'T FORGET YOUR SHOPPING BAG

WHAM!

BIFF!

BAM!

AS LONG AS I'M IMPROVING MYSELF THIS WEEK, I MIGHT AS WELL TRY TO GET ALONG WITH ODIE

JIM DAVIS 9-8

COME HERE, ODIE. GIVE ME A BIG HUG

© 1982 United Feature Syndicate, Inc.

YUK

I SHALL NOW USE SHEER WILLPOWER TO RESIST EATING THAT HAMBURGER

9-9 JIM DAVIS

UNNNGH

WAH!

I'M BEGINNING TO WORRY ABOUT GARFIELD

© 1982 United Feature Syndicate, Inc.

WHAP!

CHUKING

CATCH, GARFIELD

BONK!

EVER HAVE A DAY WHEN YOUR TIMING WAS ALL OFF?

JIM DAVIS 9-12

© 1982 United Feature Syndicate, Inc.

GIMME THAT
HAMBURGER

YOU GET A LOT MORE
ACCOMPLISHED IF YOU
DO IT WITH AUTHORITY

JIM DAVIS   9-20

© 1982 United Feature Syndicate, Inc.

9-21   JIM DAVIS

SPLAT

A VERY SHORT
BUT NEAT
RAIN SHOWER

© 1982 United Feature Syndicate, Inc.

PARDON ME. WHICH IS THE WAY TO CINCINNATI?

THANKS

I SEE BY THE OL' WRITING ON THE WALL IT'S TIME TO CHECK MYSELF INTO THE FUNNY FARM

JIM DAVIS 9-22
© 1982 United Feature Syndicate, Inc.
JIM DAVIS 9-23

© 1982 United Feature Syndicate, Inc.

LOOK AT ALL THOSE TINY ANTS GOING TO THE TINY BEACH TO DO SOME SWIMMING

UH-OH. A TINY MINNOW IS CRUISING IN TO EAT THE SWIMMERS

UH-OH. THE MINNOW JUST GOT HARPOONED BY AN ANT WHO BEARS A STRIKING RESEMBLANCE TO ROBERT SHAW

10-3

© 1982 United Feature Syndicate, Inc.

JIM DAVIS

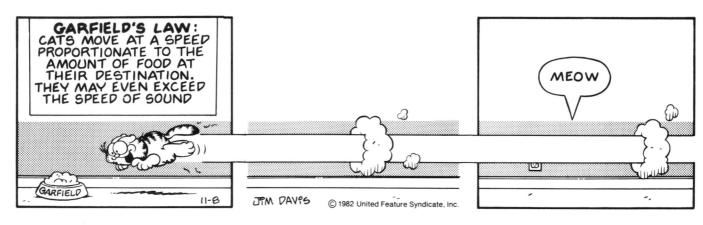

GARFIELD'S LAW: CATS MOVE AT A SPEED PROPORTIONATE TO THE AMOUNT OF FOOD AT THEIR DESTINATION. THEY MAY EVEN EXCEED THE SPEED OF SOUND

GARFIELD

11-8

JIM DAVIS

© 1982 United Feature Syndicate, Inc.

MEOW

GARFIELD'S LAW: CATS ARE INDEPENDENT. CATS ARE LONERS...

11-9

JIM DAVIS

© 1982 United Feature Syndicate, Inc.

THEY ARE UNDERFOOT ONLY WHEN YOU'RE CARRYING GROCERIES

SORRY ABOUT THAT

GARFIELD'S LAW: CATS INSTINCTIVELY KNOW THE PRECISE MOMENT THEIR OWNERS WILL AWAKE...

11-10

THEN THEY AWAKEN THEM TEN MINUTES SOONER

GARFIELD'S LAW: CATS ARE NATURALLY ATTRACTED TO ONLY ONE TYPE OF HUMAN BEING...

11-11

THE TYPE WHO IS ALLERGIC TO CATS

WAHCHOO!

GARFIELD'S LAW: CATS CAN'T HEAR COMMANDS...

GARFIELD! GET OFF THE BED!

JIM DAVIS 11-12

CATS CAN'T UNDERSTAND CAJOLING...

SEE? EVEN TOMMY THE CLOWN LIKES THIS NEW CAT FOOD

GARFIEL[

© 1982 United Feature Syndicate, Inc.

BUT THEY DO SENSE WHEN YOU WANT TO TAKE THEM TO THE VET

LET'S GO FOR A RIDE, GARFIELD

GARFIELD'S LAW: CATS SHED IN DIRECT PROPORTION TO THEIR CONTRAST WITH A PERSON'S SUIT

JIM DAVIS 11-13

© 1982 United Feature Syndicate, Inc.

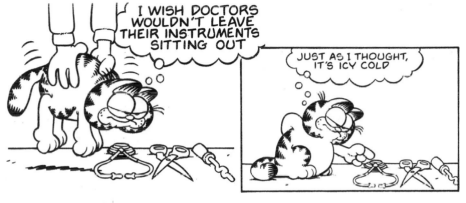

OH, GEE, I CAN'T GET INTO MY BED WITH THESE MUDDY FEET

Z

I LOVE TO SLEEP. I SLEEP TO RESTORE MY ENERGY

I SLEEP TO REFRESH MY WITS

I SLEEP TO ESCAPE

GARFIELD! WHAT HAPPENED?

I HAD A NAP ATTACK AT FULL THROTTLE

IF I WERE TO COME BACK TO THIS EARTH, I'D LIKE TO COME BACK AS A PILLOW

I COULD LIE IN BED ALL DAY

AND PEOPLE WOULD PUT THEIR HEADS IN MY LAP AND GO TO SLEEP

DON'T KNOCK THOSE FLOWERS OFF THE WINDOWSILL, GARFIELD

I PUT THEM THERE TO GIVE THEM SOME SUN

AND SOME FRESH AIR

© 1982 United Feature Syndicate, Inc.

12-6

WINDOWS ARE GREAT. THEY OFFER A FRONT ROW SEAT TO LIFE'S PASSING PARADE

JIM DAVIS 12-7

THUD!

THEY ARE ALSO GOOD FOR A YUK OR TWO

© 1982 United Feature Syndicate, Inc.

ON CHILLY MORNINGS, THIS IS MY FAVORITE PLACE IN THE WHOLE HOUSE

12-10   JIM DAVIS

OVER THE HEAT VENT

© 1982 United Feature Syndicate, Inc.

GARFIELD, DID YOU EAT MY FERN?

© 1982 United Feature Syndicate, Inc.

WHY IS IT I GET BLAMED FOR EVERYTHING AROUND HERE? IF SOMETHING GOES WRONG, YOU JUST LAY IT ON OL' GARFIELD!

12-11   JIM DAVIS

I HAVE NO IDEA WHAT YOU'RE TALKING ABOUT

GOOD MORNING, GARFIELD. IS THERE SOMETHING YOU'RE TRYING TO TELL ME?

JIM DAVIS

IT'S THE CHRISTMAS SEASON, YOU SAY

12:20

© 1982 United Feature Syndicate, Inc.

GIMME, GIMME, GIMME, GIMME, GIMME, GIMME, GIMME, GIMME

JIM DAVIS 12-21

GIMME! GIMME! GIMME! GIMME! GIMME! GIMME!

I'M GETTING INTO THE CHRISTMAS SPIRIT

© 1982 United Feature Syndicate, Inc.

NIBBLE
NIBBLE
NIBBLE

12-29

JIM DAVIS

IT'S NOT GOOD TO CHEW YOUR NAILS, GARFIELD

OH, THAT'S OKAY

I'M CHEWING ON ODIE'S

© 1982 United Feature Syndicate, Inc.

Z

JIM DAVIS

12-30

I'M BORED. I NEED TO ADD SOME SPARKLE TO MY LIFE

Z

© 1982 United Feature Syndicate, Inc.

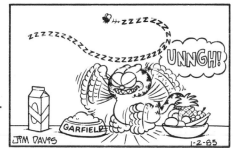

© 1983 United Feature Syndicate, Inc.

1-12 JPM DAVIS

GARFIELD, YOU SEEM TO BE PREOCCUPIED THIS WEEK

HUH?

© 1983 United Feature Syndicate, Inc.

GARFIELD HASN'T BEEN LISTENING TO ME LATELY. WATCH THIS

1-13 JPM DAVIS

HEY, GARFIELD, WHAT SAY WE GO TO THE VET AND GET YOU DECLAWED?

THAT WOULD BE FINE

CASE CLOSED

© 1983 United Feature Syndicate, Inc.

© 1983 United Feature Syndicate, Inc.

© 1983 United Feature Syndicate, Inc.

GARFIELD, SOMETIMES I THINK YOU DON'T LIKE IT WHEN I HAVE DATES

ABSOLUTELY

JIM DAVIS 1-21

DATING LEADS TO MARRIAGE. MARRIAGE LEADS TO CHILDREN

AND DO YOU KNOW WHAT CHILDREN DO TO CATS?

© 1983 United Feature Syndicate, Inc.

HEY, JON, WHAT'S HAPPENING?

JIM DAVIS

EAT YOUR BREAKFAST, GARFIELD

1-22

WHERE'S YOUR SENSE OF HUMOR?

© 1983 United Feature Syndicate, Inc.

WHIRRR!

NIGHTIE-NIGHT, JON

I HATE YOU

1-26

SURPRISE, GARFIELD! I BOUGHT YOU ANOTHER RUBBER MOUSE

YIPPEE SKIP

BY THE WAY, WHAT HAPPENED TO YOUR LAST ONE?

IT WAS TRAGIC

HE WAS CAUGHT AND EATEN BY A RUBBER CAT

1-27

© 1983 United Feature Syndicate, Inc.

JIM DAVIS 1-30

PLOP!

EEEEEEK!

JIM DAVIS 1-31

I'M ALMOST AFRAID TO ASK WHAT HAPPENED HERE

QUICK! QUICK! PUT POOKY'S ARM BACK ON!

JIM DAVIS

RELAX, GARFIELD. I'LL FIX POOKY RIGHT UP. IT'S NO BIG DEAL

2-1

NO BIG DEAL?! LOOK, BUSTER, I'VE NEVER LOST A LOVED ONE BEFORE

2-2   JIM DAVIS

I SEWED POOKY'S ARM BACK ON AS GOOD AS NEW, GARFIELD

YES, BUT WILL HE EVER PLAY THE PIANO AGAIN?

ME THINKS THE CAT DOTH EXPECT TOO MUCH

© 1983 United Feature Syndicate, Inc.

YOU DID A PRETTY GOOD JOB OF SEWING POOKY'S ARM ON

2-3   JIM DAVIS

I USED SMALL STITCHES SO AS NOT TO LEAVE A SCAR

I THINK HE'S PICKING ON ME

© 1983 United Feature Syndicate, Inc.

POOKY, WHEN YOU LOST YOUR ARM, I GOT TO THINKING ABOUT OUR MORTALITY, AND THAT'S DEPRESSING

2-4

JiM DAViS

SO PROMISE ME YOU'LL NEVER LOSE YOUR ARM AGAIN, OKAY?

I WONDER WHAT MY FORTUNE COOKIE FORTUNE IS.

JiM DAViS

2-5

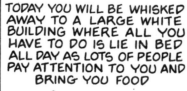
TODAY YOU WILL BE WHISKED AWAY TO A LARGE WHITE BUILDING WHERE ALL YOU HAVE TO DO IS LIE IN BED ALL DAY AS LOTS OF PEOPLE PAY ATTENTION TO YOU AND BRING YOU FOOD

THAT SOUNDS TOO GOOD TO BE TRUE

I CAN STARE ANYTHING DOWN

UH, GARFIELD, FISH CAN'T BLINK

NOW HE TELLS ME... NOW THAT MY EYEBALLS ARE ALL DRIED OUT

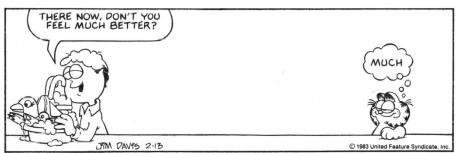

© 1983 United Feature Syndicate, Inc.

ARE YOU SURE YOU WANT TO WATCH THIS, GARFIELD?

IT'S A DEPRESSING MOVIE ABOUT A MAN-EATING LION THAT TERRORIZES A NATIVE VILLAGE

2-14

YOU ROOT FOR YOUR SIDE, I'LL ROOT FOR MINE

LION

I HATE MOVIES ABOUT MAN-EATING LIONS

HOW CAN AN ANIMAL POSSIBLY PREY ON AN INNOCENT VICTIM?

2-15

EXPLAIN THAT TO THE CHICKEN YOU HAD FOR DINNER

OH, NO! THE LION RAN DOWN ANOTHER VILLAGER!

THE ORIGINAL FAST-FOOD FRANCHISE

JIM DAVIS

NOW WHAT DISGUSTING THING IS THE LION DOING?

2-16

HE'S SPITTING THE SPEAR OUT

© 1983 United Feature Syndicate, Inc.

TELL ME WHEN THE LION IS FINISHED EATING THE VILLAGER, OKAY, GARFIELD?

YOU CAN LOOK NOW

JIM DAVIS

EEEEEK!

2-17

HE WASN'T DONE YET!

OH, I THOUGHT YOU MEANT THE MAIN PARTS

© 1983 United Feature Syndicate, Inc.

JOGGING IS MUCH MORE ENJOYABLE IF YOU HAVE THE PROPER MOTIVATION

2-23

© 1983 United Feature Syndicate, Inc.

♪ DING DING ♪

ICE CREAM

I'D BETTER SAVE SOME OF THIS BLUEBERRY PIE FOR JON. TO EAT IT ALL WOULD BE INCONSIDERATE AND SELFISH

2-24

I AM WHAT I AM

© 1983 United Feature Syndicate, Inc.

3-6

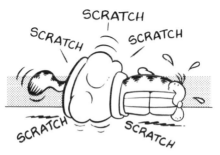

WELL, GARFIELD. HERE WE ARE IN THE GREAT OUTDOORS

IT'S OUTDOORS ALL RIGHT, BUT I'D DEBATE THE "GREAT"

JUST LISTEN TO THE SOUNDS OF NATURE

SOUNDS LIKE NOISE TO ME

3-20

JIM DAVIS

NATURE CAN ACTUALLY SPEAK TO YOU, YOU KNOW

GO ON

HEAR THAT? NATURE IS SPEAKING TO YOU NOW

WAIT, I DO HEAR SOMETHING...

I HEAR IT! I HEAR IT!

NATURE IS SAYING, "GARFIELD THE CAT, YOU'RE A LONG WAY FROM YOUR WARM BED AND TELEVISION SET"

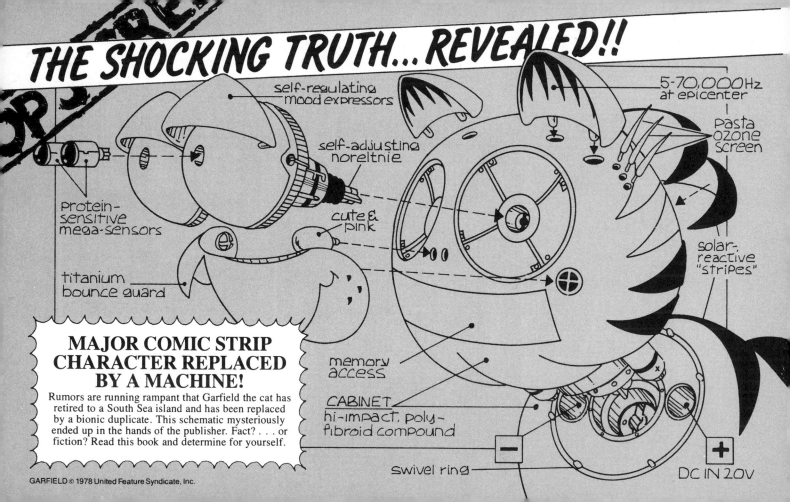

THE SHOCKING TRUTH... REVEALED!!

self-regulating mood expressors

self-adjusting noreltnie

5-70,000 Hz at epicenter

pasta ozone screen

protein-sensitive mega-sensors

cute & pink

solar-reactive "stripes"

titanium bounce guard

MAJOR COMIC STRIP CHARACTER REPLACED BY A MACHINE!

Rumors are running rampant that Garfield the cat has retired to a South Sea island and has been replaced by a bionic duplicate. This schematic mysteriously ended up in the hands of the publisher. Fact? . . . or fiction? Read this book and determine for yourself.

memory access

CABINET hi-impact poly-fibroid compound

swivel ring

DC IN 20V